W0010993

SUPERSTITIONS

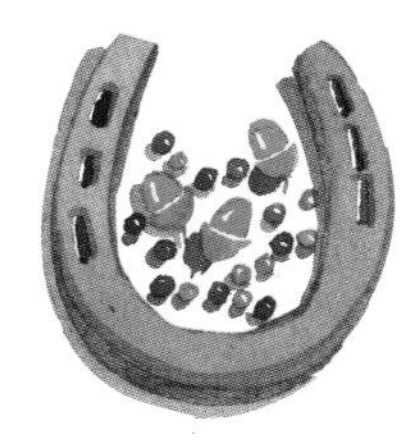

SUPERSTITIONS

LEARN WHAT TO DO WHEN YOU BREAK A MIRROR OR STEP UNDER A LADDER!

ELEANOR COOMBE

Contents

Introduction: What is Superstition?

Have you ever broken a mirror and worried you will have seven years bad luck? Perhaps you have thought something dreadful might happen on Friday the 13th. If you have touched wood, walked around a ladder or stepped over the cracks on the sidewalk to avoid misfortune, then you are showing a degree of belief in superstitions.

Why are people superstitious? Superstitions live today because people still follow beliefs and customs passed down to us from ancient times. These old beliefs or notions can still send a chill down our spines, or cheer us up and make us feel lucky, despite the fact they are often at odds with our modern education, reason or logic. For example, many of us are afraid to open an umbrella inside a house or to spill salt, yet we smile gleefully if we find a pin, because we know a rhyme that says: *"See a pin and pick it up and all the day you'll have good luck."*

"SEE A PIN AND PICK IT UP
AND ALL THE DAY YOU'LL HAVE GOOD LUCK."

Once, it was believed that objects made from iron and steel, such as pins, could keep evil spirits away, so having a lucky pin or horseshoe was security against the influences of wicked spirits and less-than-friendly witches.

Superstitious sayings and customs come from times when people believed the world was filled with such malevolent supernatural beings. Our ancestors held strong beliefs about what elements, charms, spells or mascots could protect them from these evils, and rituals and ceremonies were practiced in the hope of warding off disaster and providing a better future.

Throughout history, humans have hoped to influence their destinies and keep on the right side of the incomprehensible powers that govern their lives. Although by their nature superstitions are irrational, they are living relics of magical practices that were in existence long before the written word.

Opinions as to the validity of these beliefs vary greatly. Some people consider that all superstitions are absurd in the light of present-day knowledge, and that no sensible person should give them a second thought. Others believe that superstitions remain a vital force in our lives and a key to understanding our psyche and intellectual history. Superstitions are also studied in connection with academic disciplines, such as anthropology, archaeology, mythology and folklore, literature and heraldic symbols.

As superstitions shed light on our history and give hints into the religious rites of our ancestors, many people think it would be unwise to dismiss them lightly. There is reason to believe that many superstitions are not just silly 'wives' tales, but are often based on an older truth.

It was an old superstition to *"put honey on an ulcer to heal it."* Today, doctors are investigating whether honey has antibiotic properties. A number of modern medicines have a herbal base, such as aspirin (which comes from willow bark) and digitalis (which comes from foxgloves), while other herbal remedies alleviate such conditions as rheumatism and depression. All these cures have come from the study of ancient charms and superstitions surrounding plants.

Through most of our history, people were more intimately involved with the natural environment and the behavior of animals and plants than we are today. The study of the natural environment gave them warnings of impending storms and natural disasters. Pagan ceremonies, involving sacred wells, rivers, trees, the sun and the moon were practiced, because these natural elements affected people's lives and their influences were revered.

These ancient beliefs still lie deep in our psyche and, as our world becomes increasingly mechanized and disconnected from nature, we have to wonder if the environment has yet to teach us more lessons. Perhaps practicing superstitions and keeping the old ways alive is not so silly; and when we look more closely at superstitions, we often discover much more than whimsical notions entertained regardless of reason or logic.

Superstition Through the Ages

The Evolution of Superstitions

From our earliest days, humankind has seen the natural world as a war between dark and light, good and evil. The changes of night and day, summer and winter, fair and foul weather, were seen as conflicts among countless gods and nature spirits who, while battling one another, also fought either for or against humans.

The Sun

The sun and its movements held a great deal of awe for primitive man. When the sun was seen to weaken during winter, ceremonies were performed to encourage its regeneration. Bonfires were lit to celebrate significant times of the year, such as Beltane, Midsummer and Halloween, as these festivals heralded the transformations of the seasons and the times to plant and to harvest crops. Bonfires and firework-nights are remnants of these celebrations. The sun eventually came to be seen as divine, embodied in the form of sun gods, such as Apollo and Ra.

Many rituals and beliefs surrounded the sun and its divine gods and are still with us today. For instance, it is still considered unlucky to point at the sun. Sun flags, rising suns and sun insignias on military uniforms are all popular motifs because of an underlying belief that the wearer will be blessed with health, success and power.

As the sun rises from east and traveled westward, the east was seen as the direction associated with resurrection. It was believed to be fortunate to be born at sunrise, and unfortunate to be born at sunset. People also believed that it was good luck for anything that turned to follow the same clockwise pattern. For instance, it was lucky to stir cakes, jams and stews from east to west, or from right to left. It was believed that stirring food this way ensured excellent results and the greatest benefit to anyone eating the meals. Any dance or ceremonial turn was also performed in a clockwise direction. To go against the sun was thought very unlucky and was considered to increase the forces of darkness.

Storms

In medieval Europe, people thought the devil raised storms. There is a saying: *"Thunder is the noise of the devil cracking walnuts."* Grandmothers covered the mirrors in the house during storms, because they believed the devil might catch a person's reflection (or soul) during a lightning flash and death would come to the house.

Zeus, Jupiter, Thor and other mythological deities were all thunder gods. If a person was hit by lightning, it was considered the gods had punished them. Various plants such as oak and mistletoe were considered sacred to the thunder gods and were used as protective amulets against lightning and sorcery.

As time went on, people believed that shamans, priests, wizards, witches and other special individuals could intervene and control the supernatural powers that either healed people and made crops grow, or caused illness, death and destruction.

Superstition and Religion

People eventually developed various cultural practices that they believed could influence the powers of nature and appease the gods. To do this, people practiced daily acts of purification and used ritual objects, such as candles, floral offerings, bells and sacrifices, to ward off evil.

As people believed demi-gods, faeries and sprites inhabited rivers, woods and wild places, men rarely felled trees or crossed rivers without saying prayers or leaving offerings. Women ritually left food and gifts out for the deities, hoping in return for their blessings.

Great occasions such as births, deaths and marriages involved keeping the many supernatural powers as happy as possible. Eventually, religious institutions incorporated these ceremonies and beliefs into a more formalized structure, modifying them to suit the religion.

The moon

In ancient Europe, lucky days were attributed to the moon, especially the full moon. There were special courting moons and harvest moons. These old rites have left us the following superstitions and beliefs:

- ★ Lovers are more romantic in a full moon.
- ★ Bowing to the new moon three times is considered lucky.
- ★ A secret wish made beneath the new moon is considered lucky.
- ★ Looking at a new moon through glass is considered bad luck, as this shows disrespect.

Sacred wells and holy water

People used to visit wells to pray to the nymphs and offer them gifts by throwing valuable objects into the waters. In return, it was believed that the water nymphs would grant the gift-giver's hearts' desire or cure an illness. This popular custom continues to be practiced each time we throw coins into wishing wells. Holy springs like Lourdes in France are still dedicated to healing the sick and for protecting people from misfortune. Holy water is also used by most religions and is still supposed to have the power to dispel evil.

Bread

The eating of small wheaten cakes was once sacred to Dionysus, Adonis and Osiris. By consuming bread dedicated to these gods, devotees believed that they were partaking of the gods' divine essence.

The practice of eating dedicated bread is still observed in the Christian Communion. In medieval times, people put such faith in Communion bread that they carried it off and used it in magical charms and for healing the sick. A great deal of superstition still surrounds the eating and use of bread:

- ★ No one should sing while they make bread.
- ★ Setting a loaf upside down on the table is unlucky.
- ★ If bread is left uneaten on your plate, bad luck will follow.
- ★ For any person to take the last slice of bread from a plate is unlucky, unless the head of the table offers it to them. Then, if you are the "lucky last" and eat the offered bread, good luck in love and money will be yours.

Superstition and Social Behavior

Many of the major events in our lives are still governed by ancient beliefs. The old ways of our ancestors are unwittingly passed down to us through our social activities and during the major ceremonies in our lives.

Birthdays

Who hasn't carefully cut a birthday cake so that the knife does not touch the cake tray? Have you also made sure that you blew out all the candles with one breath? Not to accomplish these tasks at a birthday party is considered unlucky, yet the reasons we practice these rituals are lost to antiquity. The days on which we are born are also believed to affect our lives as this old rhyme tells us:

"Monday's child is fair of face
Tuesday's child is full of grace
Wednesday's child is full of woe
Thursday's child has far to go
Friday's child is loving and giving
Saturday's child works hard for a living
But the child born on the Sabbath day, is lucky, bonny, wise and gay."

Death

When a person dies, it is widely believed to be important to adhere to due ceremony, so that the soul can be transported to the afterlife. Many rituals have evolved around burials. It was once commonly believed that a corpse must leave a house, feet first, by the front door, and the body must be carried. Another very old English tradition was that the undertaker should stick pins into every gateway passed during the funeral procession, to stop evil spirits from approaching the corpse. Rain during a funeral was considered lucky for the dead person's soul. An old rhyme says:

"HAPPY IS THE BRIDE THAT THE SUN SHINES ON HAPPY IS THE CORPSE THAT THE RAIN RAINS ON."

"Happy is the bride that the sun shines on
Happy is the corpse that the rain rains on."

Some other superstitions surrounding funerals and death are:

- Walking or driving in front of a funeral procession is unlucky.
- To delay a funeral is very unlucky as this denotes more deaths in the family.
- A corpse's eyes must be closed at death, because it is believed they are looking for someone to accompany them to the grave. Coins were once put on the eyes of a dead person so they could pay the "ferryman" to carry them into the next world.
- When a corpse is laid in its coffin, it is lucky for its feet to be towards the rising sun.

Popular Superstitions

Superstitions of Kings and Queens

In early times, powerful rulers sought to enhance their influence and majesty by associating themselves with heavenly divinities, especially the sun. Various rulers regarded themselves as "sun kings." For instance, Alexander the Great assumed the title of Sun God, and the Roman emperor, Aurelian, established "The Invincible Sun" as a state religion. The Japanese emperors considered themselves to be descended from the sun goddess. The Aztecs, Incas and Mayans along with the Egyptians, also believed their royal families were descended from the sun god.

To emphasize their kinship with the sun, these rulers wore golden crowns, which symbolized the sun's rays coming from their heads. It was believed these divine crowns gave them the authority of the cosmos, and consequently power over life and death. Gold became the color and the metal of royalty because it was the color of the sun and it didn't deteriorate. Golden thrones were assembled upon which the kings and queens could sit in a superior position to mere mortals.

Many myths associated with the sun were incorporated into the superstitions surrounding royalty. In some countries, such as Thailand, it was taboo to touch a king. Should you do so, even accidentally, it could mean your death. It was rude to point or to look upon kings and queens, unless special permission was given. Kissing the feet of a king or prostrating yourself before royalty also became common practice, for to look upon their faces was to risk being blinded by their divine light.

It also became a common belief that kings, or the sign of the sun, could cure all diseases. British Kings, up until the 18th century, were considered capable of curing scrofula (tuberculosis of the lymph glands), and

King Charles II was supposed to have touched over 90,000 subjects with this aim in mind.

Kings were also supposed to be, at all times, whole and vigorous, as it was believed their health reflected the health of the land. It was also thought that if a king became ill or sickly, the country would suffer and bad times would fall upon the land. Many superstitions surrounded a king's death. It was believed terrible storms or the sight of the Aurora Borealis announced a king's death. If a bay tree were to die in England, then it meant the king would die. Shakespeare wrote in Richard II, Act II, Scene IV:

"Tis thought the king is dead, we will not stay. The bay trees in our country are all withered."

During the course of history, many strange superstitions have evolved concerning our bodies and various body parts. Many ancient gods and goddesses were believed to have powers over the body. If our ancestors were feeling unwell, they left pictures and models of their hands, feet, heads, eyes and genitalia at the various altars of their deities, in the belief that these body parts would be healed. These ancient legends left their legacies with us. In Italy, today, it is not uncommon to see gold and silver models of body parts nailed to the walls surrounding the icon of a saint.

FEET

From prehistoric times, footprints were seen as important symbols, especially those shapes similar to footprints that were found in rock. These were considered the footprints of gods. Vishnu and Buddha have left their footprints in rock, and these footprints were worshipped Holy shrines. From ancient legends and old religious rites, these following superstitions still exist in our society.

★ Lucky toes are those that have a web between them.
★ You should always put your right shoe on before the left shoe.
★ You can lame a person by putting sharp objects in their footprints.
★ An extra toe on a foot is very lucky.

FINGERS

In Greek mythology, the Goddess Rhea gave life to finger spirits, which sprang from her fingerprints when she gave birth to Zeus. These fingers were then assigned to various gods and goddesses. The ring finger was once assigned to Venus, and became the love finger. Later it was assigned to

Apollo. The index finger was assigned to Jupiter, the little finger to Mercury. The Saturn finger or middle finger became the "rude finger." The following finger superstitions still survive today:

- ★ The third finger of the left hand (ring finger) is supposed to have healing powers. If you stroke a wound with this finger, it is supposed to take away the pain and heal the wound.
- ★ A crooked little finger is a sign a person will die rich.
- ★ If people want to avert misfortune, such as the misfortune caused by breaking a mirror, looking at a new moon through glass, or telling a lie, then they should cross their fingers behind their backs.

HAIR

The hair of the goddess Isis had powers over resurrection and reincarnation, because in the myth of the rebirth of Osiris-Horus, Isis shook her hair over Osiris's body and brought him back to life. This myth extended into other legends, and a belief sprang up that the cutting of the hair of a god, goddess or hero weakened their life force. Hair in general has many intriguing superstitions, such as:

- ★ If a woman's hair grows to a low point on her forehead (a widow's peak), she will live to be a widow.
- ★ Hair should only be cut on the waxing of the moon if you want your hair to grow, or waning of the moon if you want your hair to stop growing.
- ★ To cut hair (or nails) on Good Friday or a Sunday is unlucky. An old rhyme says: "Best never be born than Sunday shorn."
- ★ When you have cut your hair and nails, you must destroy the clippings by fire because, if a witch were to find the clippings, they could be used in an evil spell against you.

The Arts and Superstition

Artists, especially actors and musicians, have many superstitions surrounding their craft.

Music from Macbeth is considered very unlucky and should never be hummed during rehearsals or behind stage. The Witches' song in particular is the unluckiest. Actors believe it is also very unlucky to speak the name of the play, Macbeth, and they usually refer to it as the "Scottish Play."

Whistling in a theatre is also considered very unlucky. Whistling may be cheerful and musical, but it is considered unlucky by people in many walks of life, such as sailors who believe that a storm could be attracted by a whistle and miners who fear that whistling down a mine may cause a cave-in.

It is bad luck to leave three lighted candles on stage or in a dressing room, for those who sit in the room with the candles will quarrel. It is also considered bad luck for an actor to look into a mirror over the shoulder of another actor. If two reflections are seen together, then misfortune will follow to the one "overlooked."

If an actor's shoes squeak when he makes an entrance onto the stage, it is considered very good for his career, but if an actor kicks his shoes off in the dressing room and they fall on their sides, this is unlucky. If they fall the right way up, this is very lucky.

Of course, it is considered very lucky to say to actors, just before they go on stage: "Break a leg."

Superstitions About the Home

Familiar household objects also attracted many strange superstitions, particularly beds, spoons, brooms and knives.

Beds

For obvious reasons, beds are closely associated with dreaming. It was once thought that beds should point from east to west, for if they point north to south, the sleeper will have nightmares.

- ★ To prevent nightmares, never turn your mattress on a Sunday or you will have bad dreams all week.
- ★ To get into bed on one side in the evening and get out the other side in the morning is unlucky. If you do, you are said to have gotten out of the bed on the wrong side and will be in a bad temper all day.
- ★ If three people together make a bed, someone will die in it within a week.

Spoons and Knives

Spoons and knives were once considered very personal possessions and also very valuable. They were often carried by their owners, and the spoon was seen as a very feminine object, while the knife was considered masculine. Here are some superstitions regarding these objects:

- ★ To drop a spoon and have it land with the bowl upwards means a surprise is coming, but should the bowl face the floor, the person who dropped it will face disappointment.
- ★ Giving a knife at a wedding is unlucky, for it could cut the marriage ties as this rhyme tells you:
  "For woe is me! such a present luckless prove,
  For knives, they tell me, always sever love."

Luck-bringing rites are performed because people believe they have accidentally upset the balance of good and evil by their actions. People have always had deep fears about doing something, that may displease the gods or the fates.

BOASTING

Boasting was considered very unlucky. The Goddess Athena turned Arachne, a young Greek maiden, into a spider for boasting that she could spin better than the Goddess. Another unlucky woman of Grecian legend was Niobe, who boasted about her twelve beautiful sons and daughters. Apollo and Artemis were angered by her pride and slew all her children with arrows.

Even today, boasting carries deep-seated superstitious fears, for it is thought dangerous to speak of good fortune or anticipate happiness, in case the gods are angered. Bragging about beauty or wealth or how clever you have been is considered very unlucky. If you wish to turn away ill fortune, because you have spoken out of turn, then you should touch wood or make the sign of a cross by crossing your fingers.

ITCHING

The idea that a sudden itching has ominous significance or foretells a future event is also a popular but silly superstition. For instance, if your left ear itches, then someone is telling lies about you, but if your right ear itches, they are speaking well of you.

If your right eye itches, then a pleasant surprise will be waiting, and conversely, if your left eye itches, disappointment awaits. An itching nose means you will be kissed, cursed or vexed, or you will shake hands with a fool.

Invisibility and Finding Gold

Other more unusual superstitions regard certain plants, which can make you invisible or help you find gold. Chicory, if cut on July 25th with a golden knife, and in perfect silence, will confer upon the person who does this successfully the power to open locks, find hidden gold and the power of invisibility.

> "FALL FREE,
> FALL FREE
> WHERE NONE
> SHALL SEE
> AND GIVE THE SAME
> GREAT GIFT TO ME."

The tiny spores of a bracken plant, or fern seed, are also reputed to make those who gather them invisible, giving the possessor the power over all living things. However, to be effective, the fern seed has to be gathered exactly at midnight on the Eve of St John, using a silver bowl placed under the plant so as to collect a seed that was not shaken from the fern. The person seeking this form of power has to then hide the seed on their person and recite the following words:

"Fall free, fall free
Where none shall see
And give the same
Great gift to me."

Love and Harmony

Enhancing your Chances at Love

Various old traditions and charms to enhance your chances of love exist, many of them surrounding plants found in the garden or forest. Myrtle is a plant that is traditionally associated with love, and it is commonly used in bridal bouquets. Young girls made a tea from myrtle leaves to increase their beauty. It is still believed that if you give a tea made from myrtle flowers to a lover, it is a sure way of getting and keeping his or her love.

Peas also have a strange ability to secure love. If a single girl finds nine peas in a pod, she must put the pod on the lintel of the front door, and the first man to cross the threshold will be her future love. Should you want to know who would be the last person in your social circle to marry, then gather several friends together, fill a small bowl with peas, then take turns in eating one pea at a time. The person who eats the last pea will be the last to marry.

For a boy wishing to gain a girl's love, he must take an orange and prick it all over in the pits of its skin with a needle, then sleep with it under his armpit. On the next day, he must give it to the girl of his desire and see if she eats it. If she does, she'll return his love.

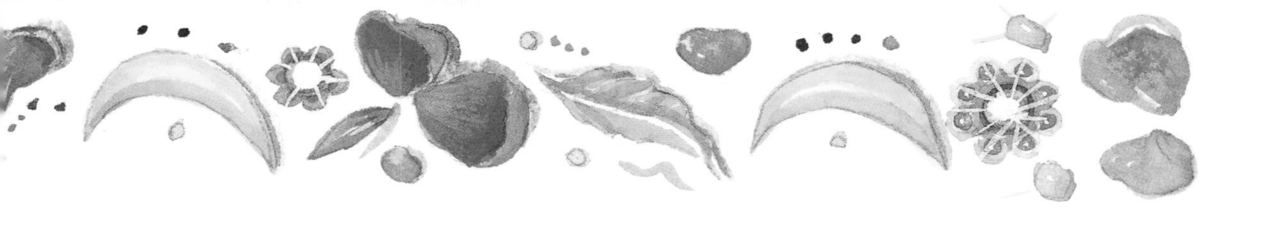

Holly and ivy, at one time sacred to Thor, Zeus and Bacchus, were believed to have magical powers and were used in a number of love-related spells. To make sure you dream of a future lover, go out on a Friday and gather nine holly leaves, without talking or making a sound. Tie the nine leaves in a three-cornered handkerchief. Tie the handkerchief with nine knots. Put the handkerchief under your pillow. Your future lover will appear in a dream, but only if you have managed to keep silent from the time you set out to fetch the leaves until you wake the following day. With ivy, take a leaf from the plant and put it against your heart, saying the following words:

"Ivy, Ivy I love you
In my bosom I put you
The first young man/woman who speaks to me
My future husband/wife he/she shall be."

"IVY, IVY I LOVE YOU
IN MY BOSOM I PUT YOU
THE FIRST YOUNG
MAN/WOMAN WHO
SPEAKS TO ME
MY FUTURE
HUSBAND/WIFE HE/SHE
SHALL BE."

Love and The Seasons

From ancient times, the moon has had a great deal of influence over the world of lovers. The year was traditionally broken up into twelve moons, with every full moon a courting moon.

Winter

Try this love spell at the first full moon of winter if the moon is shining strongly enough to cast a shadow. Take a silver bowl and fill it with water. Take a new silk handkerchief, and look at the moon's reflection in the water in the bowl through the handkerchief. The number of moons you can see will be the same as the months before your wedding day.

At the end of winter, St Valentine's Day was celebrated to cheer young lovers. Saint Valentine's Day was also the day when it was thought that the birds began to build their nests. Young girls went to churchyards on St Valentine's Eve to create charms, by running around the church three times at midnight. It was thought the girl would then dream of her future lover.

Spring

In spring, the hawthorn flowered, and this flower in particular was used in many love divinations, especially on May Eve. You might try this charm using hawthorn should you wish to attract a lover:

Hang a flowering hawthorn branch on a sign post at a crossroad on May Eve. Let it hang there all night. Return in the morning, seeing which way it has been blown by the wind. Your future lover will come from that direction. If the branch is blown away, you will never marry.

Summer

Midsummer's Eve (June 23rd, or St John's Eve) was an exciting festival when young people leapt through bonfires at night and decorated their homes with flowers made from roses, rosemary and lavender. This festival brought on a frenzy of divination for lovers. Try the following charm to help you see your future lover:

To be married within the year, gather some St John's Wort very early in the morning of St John's Eve. You must do this while you are still fasting (before breakfast), and the plant must still be covered in dew. Sleep with it under your pillow, and you will dream of the person you will marry.

Autumn

Autumn was harvest time, as well as the time for processions and fertility jokes. Country lads and lasses found amorous adventures when they went "nutting." Nuts were always symbolic of life and fertility in pagan times. In Germany the phrase "going a nutting," means "love making" and, perhaps because of this, the devil became associated with nuts. An old rhyme says:

"The devil, as the common people say,
Doth go a-nutting on Holy rood day;
And sure such lechery in some doth lurk
Going a-nutting do the devil's work."

"The devil, as the common people say,
Doth go a-nutting on Holy rood day; And sure such lechery in some doth lurk
Going a-nutting do the devil's work."

Halloween was also known as "Nutcrack Night." Try this Halloween love charm on Halloween night (31st of October). Go to your bedroom and light two candles on your dressing table. Then stand in silence before your mirror, brush your hair and eat an apple. The spirit of your future lover will be seen in the glass, looking over your shoulder.

Love Charms

Many kinds of love charms exist, using acorns, gems, mirrors, the moon, cherries, arrows, keys and fish because these objects are all associated with various love gods and goddesses. For example, an amethyst is considered a fortunate gem to give to a lover because it was thought that St Valentine wore an amethyst.

Cupid, the son of Aphrodite, is sacred to lovers. Little Cupid amulets with their bows and arrows are worn as jewelry, or sometimes just an arrow is carried as a love talisman. An amulet showing Cupid's arrow piercing two hearts and binding them together is a common love charm. Sometimes Cupid leaves his arrows behind and carries a burning torch with which he lights the fire of love. A burning torch is also a lucky charm for lovers.

"EVEN, EVEN ASH
I PLUCK THEE
OFF THIS TREE
FOR THIS NIGHT MY
TRUE LOVE I'LL SEE."

How will I see my future love?

Here are a few charms for lovers who wish to see their future lover. During a full moon, stand upon a stone on which you have never stood on before, with a mirror in your hand. Turn your back to the moon, holding up the mirror so you can see the moon in the glass. You should see a number of small moons, each one representing the number of years before your wedding.

For another charm, find an ash leaf with equal divisions on either side. Say the following words, then sleep with the leaf under your pillow to see your future love in a dream:

"Even, even ash
I pluck thee off this tree
For this night my true love I'll see."

WHO WILL BE MY LOVER?

Stick the pips from an apple on your cheek, naming each one of them for each of your potential lovers. Sit quietly and still and wait for the pips to fall off. The one that stays the longest will be the one named for your lover. If you have lots of suitors and you can't choose one, scratch their names on some onions and set them in a warm place. The onion that sprouts first will give you the name of the one you should choose as your true love.

DOES YOUR LOVER LOVE YOU?

Young girls used to perform this unhygienic love spell to find out if they were loved. They took sprigs of yarrow and put them inside their nostril, twirling the yarrow around while saying:

"Yarroway, Yarroway, bear a white blow
If my love loves me, my nose will bleed now.
If my love doesn't love me, it won't bleed a drop."

A much nicer way of finding out if you are loved is to make yourself sneeze on a particular day before eating:

"Sneeze on Sunday morning fasting,
Enjoy your true love everlasting."

Once you have been lucky enough to find your true love, some courtship superstitions should be considered. Giving roses to someone you love has been in fashion for thousands of years and is still popular. Roses were once sacred to Aphrodite and Venus. Each type of rose carries a special message, so if you are thinking of giving roses, then be sure you give the right "rose-message" to your love:

- ★ A red rose means you are pure and lovely.
- ★ A white rose means you are a virgin or a person ignorant of love.
- ★ A full-blown rose means secrecy.
- ★ A yellow rose means jealousy and a decrease of love.

If you are worried your one true love may not marry you, pluck a rosebud on Midsummer's day and wrap it in white paper. Put it away until Christmas Day, and if it is then fresh and sweet, you will marry. If it has faded and turned brown, the omen is bad.

To see if your lover really loves you, take two acorns and give one your name and the other the name of the person you love. Drop both acorns together into a bowl of water. If they float together, you will be lovers. If they float apart, your love has no hope. However, if you find two teaspoons on your saucer, it means you will be married shortly.

There are many superstitions regarding color and the courtship game. Blue is the color of Venus, Aphrodite and Isis, and is a color associated with love

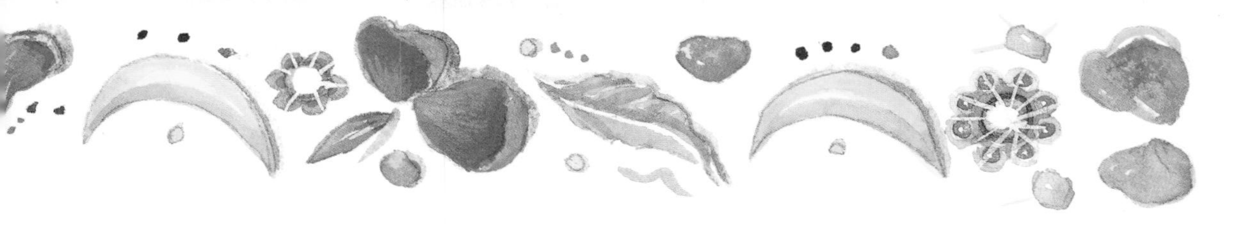

and happy lovers. These old rhymes give a clue to your lucky colors to wear when courting:

"If you love me, love me true
Send me a ribbon, a ribbon of blue.
If you hate me, let it be green
Send me a ribbon a ribbon of green."
"Those dressed in blue
Have lover's true.
In green and white
Forsaken quite."

A sprig of rosemary was also a famous mascot for lovers who were parted from each other. Rosemary meant remembrance, and the sprig had the power to keep the sender in the loved one's thoughts. So, if your true love has to go away, give them a sprig of rosemary so they will remain faithful.

St Valentine's Day is the most famous day of all for courting couples. Roses, cards, chocolates and romantic gifts are still given on St Valentine's Day. One romantic superstition consisted of a gift of gloves. If a girl received a gift of gloves from an admirer, this was a sure sign that the young man liked her. Another quaint custom was for young girls to go out on St Valentine's morning and accost the first young man she met with these words:

"Good morrow Valentine, I go today,
To wear for you what you must pay,
A pair of gloves next Easter Day."

"GOOD MORROW
VALENTINE,
I GO TODAY,
TO WEAR FOR YOU
WHAT YOU MUST PAY,
A PAIR OF GLOVES
NEXT EASTER DAY."

The times and seasons for weddings were once taken very seriously, with some months and days considered unlucky.

"Marry in May and rue the day" was an old rhyme that embodied a tradition dating back to ancient Rome, when May was a time Romans mourned the dead, and so was not a good time to take a wife. "Marry in Lent and live to repent" came from a time when the church prohibited marriages during Lent or Easter. To marry on other holy days is still considered an ill omen for marriages, especially Sundays.

GOING TO THE WEDDING

The bride is supposed to leave her home by stepping out her parent's front door with her right foot first. On the way to the wedding, it is lucky for the sun to shine on her, or for her to see a rainbow. It is very unlucky to meet a pig or a funeral. If the bride travels in a horse and carriage and the horses refuse to start, this is a bad omen. Similarly, if a wedding car doesn't start straight away, this is also considered to be unlucky.

THE WEDDING DRESS

Because the bride is entering a new stage of her life, it is thought to be lucky if her wedding dress is newly made. The only exclusion to the rule should be "something borrowed" and "something old". It is considered unlucky for a bride to make her own dress.

If a bride wishes to inspect herself in a mirror before the wedding, without causing bad luck, then she should leave one item off, or one stitch undone. Then when she is happy with her looks, she can complete her wedding attire in safety. Once a wedding is over, it is considered lucky for the bride and groom to stand side by side and look into a mirror.

Concerning the color of the wedding dress, nowadays, most colors are acceptable to brides, but not so long ago a bride could only be seen in white, as this was the color of virginity. The tradition of wearing white began in the 16th century. In earlier times, blue was popular, as it is the color of love, and even today, "something blue" should always be included in the wedding attire.

THE VEIL

The word "revelation" comes from a Latin word meaning "to draw back the veil." The lifting of the wedding veil symbolized the secrets of womanhood that were about to be "revealed." So lifting the veil and kissing the bride was rich in sexual symbolism.

In some cultures, it was considered unlucky for the groom to see the bride before the wedding vows were finalized, so the veil covered the bride's face until then. A borrowed veil is considered luckier to wear than a new veil, especially if it has been borrowed from a happily married woman.

THE WEDDING CAKE

The cake symbolized fertility and good fortune. It is a superstition that the bride must always cut the first slice of cake, or the couple will be childless. Usually both partners cut the cake together but with the groom's hands over those of the bride.

All the guests should eat some cake. To refuse to eat the wedding cake is very unlucky, both for the bridal pair and the person who didn't taste the cake. Eating the wedding cake carefully was important

as often a ring was hidden in the cake. The lucky person who found the ring was ensured of happiness for a year. A popular belief is that if an unmarried woman places a piece of wedding cake under her pillow she will dream of her future husband.

THE RING

The wedding ring symbolizes eternal love. It is put on the third finger of the left hand because a tradition tells of a love vein, which goes from that finger to the bride's heart. If a wedding ring falls from the finger of the bride, this means bad luck for the marriage. If the ring is dropped during the ceremony, it is also unlucky, even more so if the ring rolls away from the altar steps.

THE HONEYMOON

The word "honeymoon" comes from the ancient German custom of drinking honey mead after a wedding, from the full moon to the waning of the moon. The idea that the couple should go away on a "honeymoon" came from another custom in which the groom used to ceremonially kidnap the bride and hide her away from her parents for several days.

On the first night of the honeymoon, the bridesmaids undressed the bride and prepared the wedding bed. Whoever secured a pin from the bride's dress would be the next to marry. It was also believed that the first person in a new marriage to buy a new item would be the dominant partner. Quite often, the bride would purchase some small item from the bridesmaids on the first night of her honeymoon.

After the wedding, the bride must enter her new home through the front door and be carried by the groom, in case she should fall while entering the new house. To fall would mean bad luck for the marriage.

Birth Superstitions

Anxiety has always surrounded childbirth, even more so in older times when the health and hygiene standards were not as high as those of today. As many births occurred in the home, the midwife usually unlocked all doors and loosened all knots as soon as she arrived. This was a form of magic used against evil witches, who were supposed to cause difficult births by tying knots during a woman's labor. This myth probably came from the legends of Greece, when the birth of Hercules (son of Zeus) was delayed by Zeus's jealous wife Hera, when she tied magical knots to prevent Hercules's birth. Midwives also drove nails and pins into the bedposts to keep away evil demons and fairies that might cause death or problems for the woman in labor.

Many beliefs emerged that tried to explain the high mortality rate in the first year of childbirth, along with other unfortunate events such as malformations and infirmities. Luck-bringing rituals were practiced during the first year of a child's life to try to keep the baby safe from evil sprits. Here are some more of the old superstitions regarding childbirth and pregnancy.

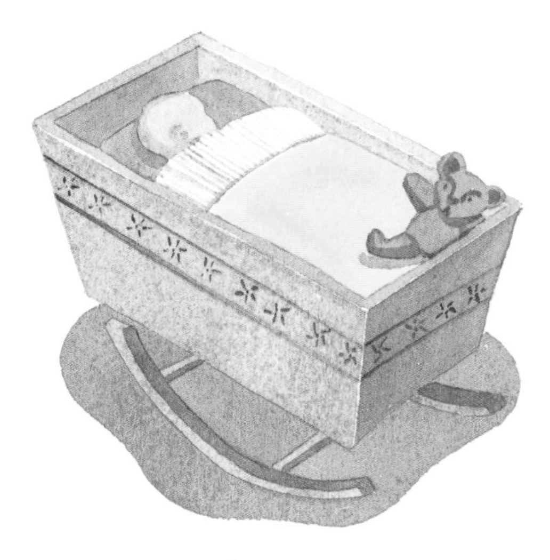

- ★ If your apron falls off, you will be pregnant within the year.
- ★ To rock an empty cradle means you will get pregnant soon.
- ★ If a pregnant woman meets a hare, then her baby will be born with a "hare-lip".
- ★ If a witch touches a woman during pregnancy, birthmarks will appear on her baby.
- ★ A pregnant woman must never walk near the plant cyclamen, because to do so would endanger her and could cause a miscarriage.
- ★ If a child is born feet first, he or she will have magical or healing powers.
- ★ If a baby is born with a caul over his or her face, he or she will be lucky and rich.
- ★ Good Friday births are unlucky, and such a child will have sadness all his or her life.
- ★ Babies born in May are weak and sickly and never do well.
- ★ Newborn babies are in danger from the fairies until their first sneeze.
- ★ Mothers should never cut their babies' nails, but should nibble the nails off and swallow them until the child is twelve months old.
- ★ If a baby's first tooth appears on the lower jaw, this means he or she will have a long life.
- ★ A baby should not see itself in the mirror until six months old. It is very unlucky before this time.
- ★ Children born by caesarian section are supposed to be strong all their days and have the power to find hidden treasure and see spirits.
- ★ The top tier of the parent's wedding cake should be kept for the christening celebration when the first child is born.

"TIS NOT THESE PINS
I WISH TO BURN,
BUT (LOVER'S NAME) I
WISH TO TURN.
MAY (HE/SHE) NEITHER
SLEEP NOR REST,
TILL (HE/SHE) HAS
GRANTED MY REQUEST."

HOW TO KEEP YOUR LOVE

Not all romances run smoothly, and faithless lovers have broken many hearts. The following superstitions tell of ways to keep your lover.

To recall a faithless lover: throw twelve new pins on a fire at midnight and say:

"Tis not these pins I wish to burn,
But (lover's name) I wish to turn.
May (he/she) neither sleep nor rest,
Till (he/she) has granted my request."

Or you may like to try this traditional spell by gathering three roses on Midsummer's Night Eve. In the small hours of the following morning, bury one under a yew-tree and another in a newly-made grave. Place the third rose under your pillow. Leave it there for three nights, then burn it. You will then haunt your lover's dreams until he or she returns to you.

To complete this spell, you will need to collect an oak leaf, twig and acorn, and some ash keys (which are the seeds of the ash tree) and put them under your pillow for three nights in a row, repeating these words each night:

"Acorn cup and ashen key,
Bid my true love come to me –
Between moonlight and firelight,
Bring him/her over the hills tonight
Over the meadows, over the moor,
Over the rivers, over the sea,
Over the threshold of my door,
Acorn cup and ashen key,
Bring my true love back to me."

Will they come back?

To know whether your ex-love will return to you, place seven beans in a circle on the road along which your ex-lover walks. If he or she treads in the circle or on the beans, he or she will return to you. If he or she misses the beans, your love is doomed.

Wear a moonstone as a charm to help you reconcile with a parted lover.

How to check your lover will be faithful

Put an apple pip on a grate before the fire. Name the pip for the one you love. If the person loves you, it will bounce and fly. If the person doesn't love you, it will sit there and shrivel up and burn. If it bursts, your lover will be faithful.

Another superstition requires you to wait until your lover walks on soft ground. Secretly dig the earth from your lover's footprint. Put the earth in a pot and sow marigold seeds in the earth. When they grow, you will be sure of his or her love.

To ensure that you will not turn your sweetheart away, don't turn your mattress on a Friday. If you wish to make your love stay true to you, steal your lover's garter and tie three lover's knots in it. Say the following words:

"Three times a true love's knot
I tie secure:
Firm be the knot, firm may his
love endure."

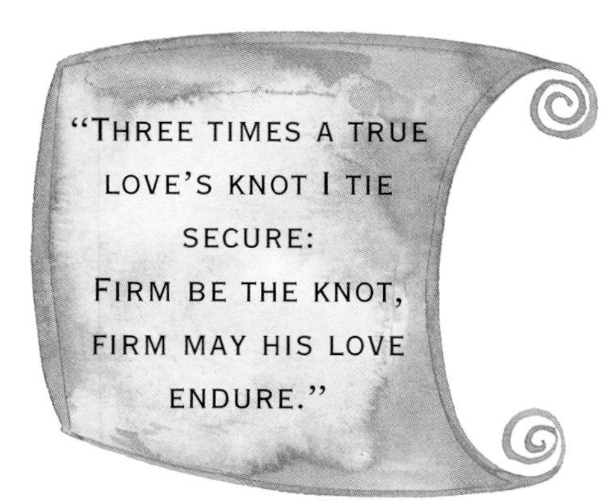

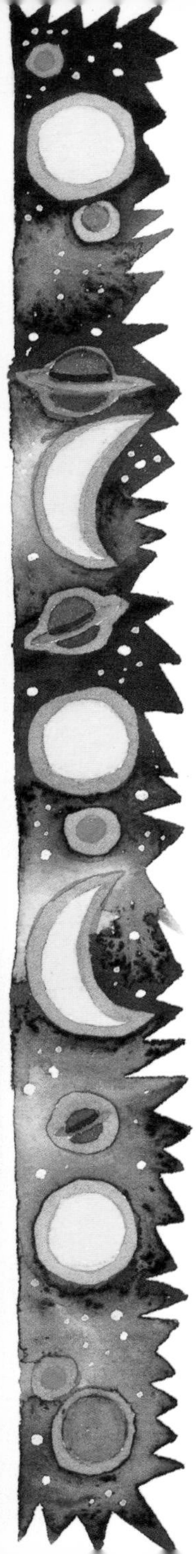

Feeling Lucky

Good Luck Superstitions

Since the beginning of time, humans have looked to amulets, talismans and charms to bring them luck, ward off evil, and attract wealth, health, love and long life. Magical powers were linked to various objects, such as a rabbit's foot or a four-leaf clover, and people felt empowered to use those charms as protection against ill fortune. There were other charms, which had certain rules associated with them, such as magical spells, secret writings or blessed and sacred objects.

Charms and spells were sold and traded, and people wore charms and amulets to attract the gods' approval. It was believed that wearing sacred charms showed the gods that you were a devout person and worshipped righteously. People still carry a crucifix, crescent, or Star of David because they show a loyal connection with the Almighty.

Even today, it is believed that sacred objects can ward off evil. Many movies show how a crucifix can ward off the devil vampires and other malevolent entities.

Sacred mandalas are used for bringing luck in China, Tibet and India, and are now accepted as lucky symbols worldwide. The mandala is usually drawn, painted or made from sand. Mandalas are "cosmograms" created to help with meditation and aid in creating harmony, world order and the cosmic balance of good and evil.

Lucky moon

The moon was the most important heavenly body in the sky next to the sun. Its mysterious waxing and waning created many myths and legends. The changes in the moon were also seen as similar to life and death and resurrection. The new moon was always venerated as a symbol of rebirth and luck with money and health.

Housewives used to turn their aprons and make a secret wish when they saw a new moon. As long as they didn't tell anyone what they wished for, their wish was supposed to come true.

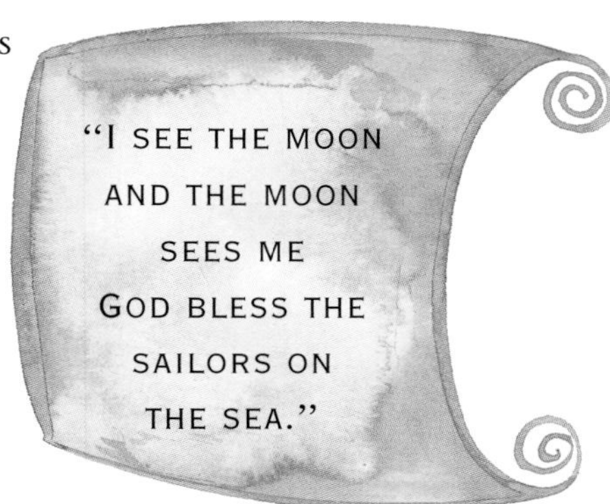

On the sight of the new moon, the family and friends of seamen would chant:

"I see the moon and the moon sees me
God bless the sailors on the sea."

SALT

Salt was used as a charm against evil since the earliest days. This is probably because with no refrigeration, salt was highly prized for preserving food. Because salt preserved things from decay, it was held as a symbol of eternity. Salt, traded across Europe and was also very expensive. The Roman army often paid its troops with salt. Consequently, if salt was spilled accidentally, it was considered very unlucky; the only way to counter such bad luck was to throw some of the spilled salt over your shoulder to frighten away the invisible, evil spirit that stood behind you.

To bring luck into a new house, people thought that one of the first things to be carried inside should be a box of coal and a plate of salt.

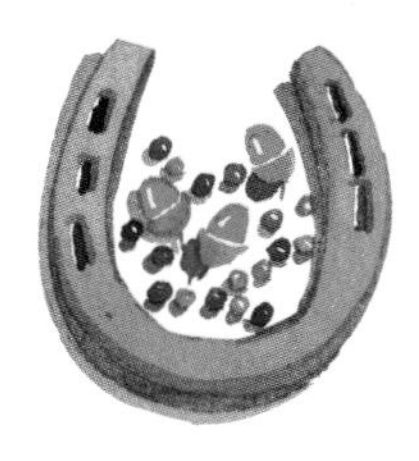

How to Attract Good Luck

In general, a person who lives a good life expects to be rewarded. A good life attracts good luck. It use to be believed that gods and goddesses enjoyed playing with our lives, and some people were favored at birth by the whim of a god, or born under a lucky star, and so attracted good luck automatically.

Even though people lived good lives, there was a belief that evil creatures could maliciously harm anyone who didn't practice special luck-bringing ceremonies. It was believed that burning candles or incense, or ringing bells, or carrying special stones or blessed charms could drive away bad thoughts and evil demons, and could take prayers and blessings to the heavens.

People believed that certain colors were blessed with happiness or luck, or that numbers carried magical significance. Lucky numbers were linked with zodiac signs, carrying mystical luck with them for those born on certain days and for gamblers. Numbers with multiples of three were often used in magical love spells because three was a sacred number:

- ★ One is the number for the sun and is lucky for Leo and Aries.
- ★ Two is ruled by the moon. It is lucky for Gemini and Pisces and is the number for good wishes, second sight and joy.
- ★ Three is ruled by Jupiter and is probably the luckiest number, and is held sacred by most religions. It is fortunate for anyone born in Sagittarius.
- ★ Four is also a sun number, bestowing healing powers and worldly success, and is the number for those born under Leo.

* ★ Five is the number for Mercury and is lucky because it bestows energy, activity, ambition, warmth and love, especially to those born under Gemini and Virgo.
* ★ Six is the number of Aphrodite or Venus and is associated with love, partnership and harmony. It is lucky for Libra and Taurus.
* ★ Seven is for the seven days, seven colors, the seven gifts of the spirit, wisdom, honor, understanding, glory, blessing, strength and godliness. It is the number of magic and is lucky for Cancer.
* ★ Eight rules old age, death, time and space. It is the number of justice and the number of Saturn. Saturn rules both Aquarius and Capricorn.
* ★ Nine is ruled by Mars, and is lucky for those born under the sign of Scorpio. Nine was also the sign of the nine fates or faeries, and the number was considered very lucky. Nine is used in many charms as it is three times three, and so is three times fortunate.

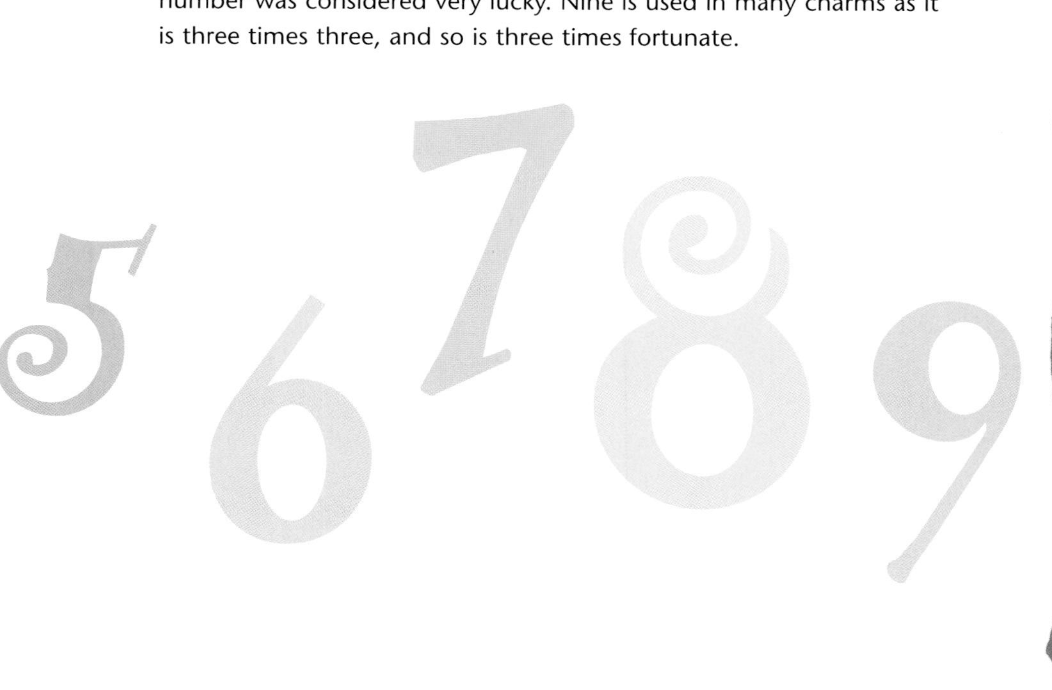

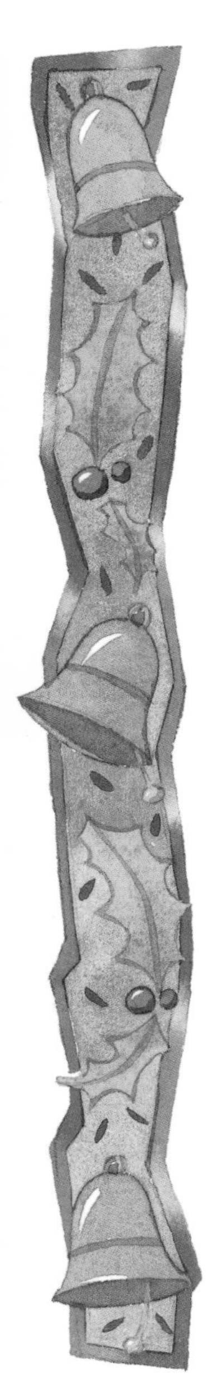

Simple actions were married to simple spoken formulas. They were easily remembered and passed down from generation to generation unchanged. For instance, a "sigil" was a mystical charm, sign or magical word, which was usually carried in a little bag or in a locket around the neck. Sometimes these sigils were carved items of jewelry.

One of the most powerful sigils was supposed to have been the word "Abracadabra." It was written on a piece of paper and worn for nine days, then thrown over the left shoulder into a stream. The letters in the charm had to be written in the form of an inverted triangle:

ABRACADABRA
BRACADABR
RACADAB
ACADA
CAD
A

The meaning of the word "Abracadabra" remains mysterious, but it is believed to bring good luck and help healing. Stage magicians still use the word when performing magic tricks.

The hexagram, also a lucky charm, was formed by two interlocking triangles. The symbol protects against fire, deadly weapons and the perils of travel.

Sneezes were also considered lucky and warded off evil, an old chant says:
"Sneeze on a Monday,
You get a letter.
Sneeze on a Tuesday,
You get something better.
Sneeze on a Wednesday,
You sneeze for danger.
Sneeze on a Thursday,
Meet a stranger.
Sneeze on a Friday,
Sneeze for sorrow.
Sneeze on a Saturday,
See your best friend tomorrow."

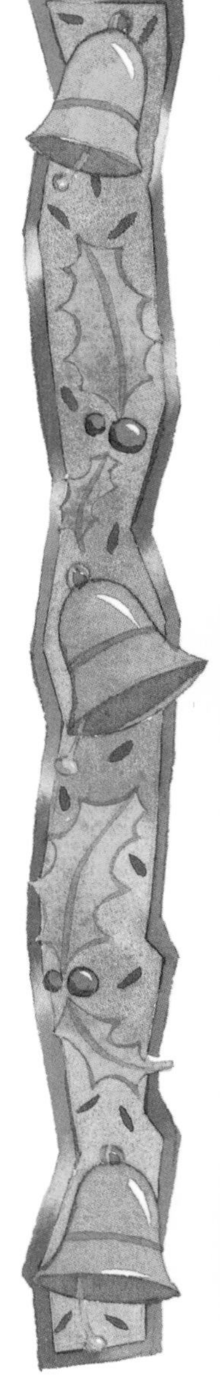

LUCKY CLOTHES AND SHOES

Garments enclose the body, and it was always the impression that clothes captured the "aura" of the wearer. Therefore, it was believed the robe of a saint, prophet or famous person would give anyone who owned it certain powers. Scraps of saint's clothing were believed to have miraculous powers, and charlatans sold endless scraps of "sacred clothing" or "sacred shrouds" as lucky charms.

Clothes worn by famous people are still considered very valuable and are highly sought after as mascots or collectibles. So, it is not very far-fetched to think that an ordinary person's clothes also have certain magical powers. These old superstitions have been handed down to us concerning our clothes.

- ★ If you accidentally put your clothes on inside out, this is very lucky. But you mustn't change them or you will change your luck.
- ★ If you put on new clothes for the first time, make a wish. If there is a pocket, put a coin in it to ensure plenty of money for the future.
- ★ When children wear new clothes, they should be pinched while the following chant is recited:

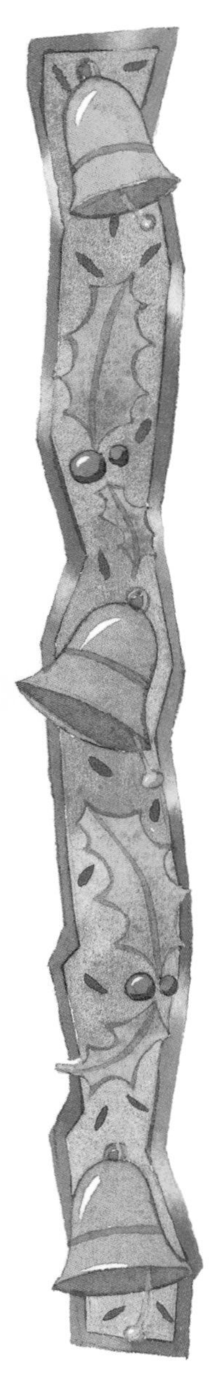

"HEALTH TO
WEAR IT
STRENGTH TO
TEAR IT
AND MONEY TO BUY
ANOTHER."

"Health to wear it
Strength to tear it
And money to buy another."

It is lucky to put shoes at the end of your bed at night, in the shape of a T, and with soles uppermost. This prevents cramps and nightmares.

Sacred possessions of gods and goddesses also had luck associated with them. People adapted the god's possessions into lucky amulets and charms and wore them for protection. The ankh, the symbol of life, was also the hand mirror of Hathor and Venus. It was considered to be a very lucky symbol, as it was believed to attract good health and fertility, and to strengthen psychic powers.

Silver was dedicated to Isis and in Mexico it was called "the silver excrement of the gods." Many charms were made of silver because it was considered very lucky, especially when associated with the moon. Silver sixpences were given to people for luck, and silver charms warded off demons. Silver bullets killed werewolves, and silver arrows or bullets could kill storm witches if they were fired into dark clouds.

Horseshoes, like pins, are made of metal, and therefore have the power to frighten away evil spirits. Horseshoes are considered to be particularly lucky charms, bringing good fortune and protecting the house from evil spirits. Some superstitions say the horseshoe should always be hung upright above a door, as if to hold the good fortune in its curve, but others say it should be nailed downwards, possibly symbolizing a protective covering around the shape of the door to prevent evil from entering. Either way, the horseshoe should be nailed up with three nails.

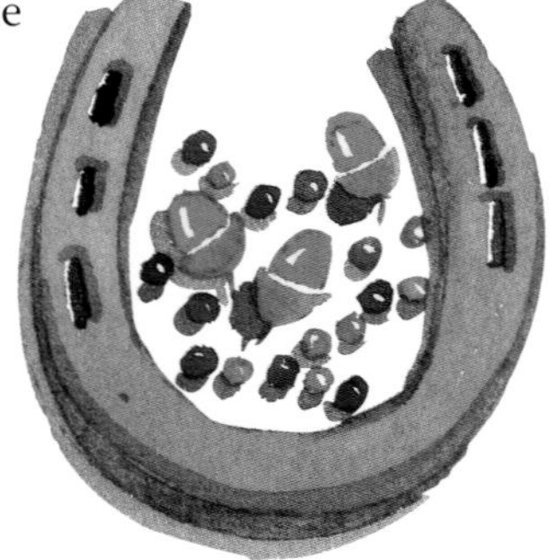

St John's Wort, or hypericum, was another lucky plant that was dedicated to St John. It kept malevolent witches away, and combined with other sacred plants, such as clover, vervain and dill, made a powerful charm.

"Trefoil, vervain, John's Wort and dill
Hinder witches of their will."

St John's Wort also made an excellent charm against demons on Midsummer's Night and promoted well-being and fertility.

Many other plants were considered lucky too, especially rushes. In Ireland lucky rushes are still gathered on St Bride's eve. Of course, lucky rushes can't be cut with any iron tool because this may frighten away the good fairies. These rushes are taken to church and blessed, then hung over the doors of houses, beds and stables to bring good luck and protection.

To bring good luck for the New Year, boys carried evergreen branches and vessels full of water from house to house, sprinkling the rooms and its occupants with water shaken from the branches. As they went, they sang the following verse:

"Here we bring new water, from the well so clear,
For to worship God with, this Happy New Year;
Sing levy dew, sing levy dew, the water and the wine,
With seven bright gold wires, that bugles that do shine,
Sing reign of fair maid, with gold upon her toe,
Open you the west door, and turn the old year go,
Sing reign of fair maid, with gold upon her chin,
Open you the east door and let the New Year in."

Protection Against Evil

The Evil Eye

Protection against evil, disaster and disease has been sought from the heavens since man first walked upon the earth. This extract from a wonderful ancient hymn to Ishtar, the Babylonian Venus, was written over 4,000 years ago, so the people who prayed to her would be protected from evil spells:

"Thy ways are just and holy; thou dost gaze on sinners with compassion,
And each morn leadest the wayward to the rightful path.
Now linger not, but come! O Goddess fair,
When thou stoopest o'er the dying with compassion, lo! They live,
And when the sick behold thee they are healed.
Hear me, thy servant! Hearken to my pray'r, for I am full of sorrow,
And I sigh in sore distress. Be merciful my lady, pity take.
How long must my heart sorrow and make moan,
How long must my dark home be filled with mourning and my soul with grief?
O lioness of heaven, bring me peace and rest and comfort.
Hearken to my pray'r! May thine eyes look down with tenderness and blessings,
And behold thy servant.
Oh! Have mercy; hear my cry and un-bewitch me from the evil spells."

Prayers, rituals and ceremonial magic were used to rid people of evil ghosts, demons, troublesome spirits and the evil eye. All over the world, people believe in the evil eye. The eye has long been considered capable of issuing beams of light and spiritual expression. At a glance, an eye can cast a message of love or hate. Evil creatures were thought to have gazes that rendered people powerless, or even turned them to stone, as in the case of the feared gaze of Medusa. Perseus eventually killed Medusa with the aid of a mirrored bronze shield.

In Celtic legend, the terrifying Formorian King, Balor, had a giant eye. His evil gaze worked when four men lifted his eyelid and he gazed at his enemy and destroyed them. His evil gaze was destroyed by Lugh, using a stone fired by a slingshot.

Angry or envious looks even from a very ordinary person were feared, and it was thought ill fortune would come of those gazes. Certain magical individuals were believed capable of bringing misfortune or illness to animals and people and damage to household goods just by looking at them. The term "overlooked" came into being, and was applied to people who had fallen beneath some enchantment. The feared gaze of the evil eye led people to create many amulets to protect them from these terrible emanations.

Although those with an evil eye could transmit evil, good luck was also associated with the eye. The sun was known as the "all seeing eye" and associated with powerful and protective sun gods. The eye of Horus/Osiris was associated with regeneration, health and prosperity, and the sun's eye was considered a lucky amulet to be worn as protection against the evil eye. Blue beads and artificial blue eyes were created to keep wearers safe, and are still common charms found all through the Middle East and Turkey.

Malevolent witches also were considered to have "the evil eye" and these witches could also turn themselves into hares, toads or black cats. Therefore, having one of these creatures crossing your path was considered very unlucky. People felt they could avoid the evil eye and such unlucky experiences in various ways, such as making a cross with their fingers or spitting upon the roadside.

Holly, rue, oak and mistletoe were associated with the thunder gods and were considered a powerful protection against malevolent witches, demons and the evil eye. These plants were hung in the house to protect people from lightning and evil. An acorn charm was also worn to bring luck and prosperity, and give protection against lightning and the evil eye.

Amber also had a strong affinity with electricity, and it was an old Greek legend that said that amber was formed by the tears of the sun nymphs (Heliads) when they wept. In the Baltic, amber was called the tears of Freya.

Amber was reputed to cure many diseases, and amulets made of amber are supposed to repel the evil eye.

Sprigs of rue, fashioned in silver, were worn as protective amulets, and the casting of salt upon the ground or in the house created a barrier against harm. Red threads, knotted nine times, were also used as protection against evil.

Horns, or horn-shaped objects, were always considered lucky, as they had the power to bring good fortune and prosperity, as well as counter the effects of the evil eye. Horns were animals' weapons and as such they represented strength and aggressiveness. Horns were frequently seen on pictures of various deities, such as Hathor, the Egyptian goddess of heaven, who had the head of a cow. Etruscans built horn-shaped icons into their architecture, especially on the corners of their houses, for good luck and to frighten away evil. People still make the sign of the horn with their hands to avert the evil eye, using the index finger and the little finger pointing upwards in an otherwise clenched fist.

AVOIDING BAD LUCK

Doing the wrong thing can easily create bad luck; therefore, it is always wise to live cautiously and prudently. It was believed, in the past that the gods were angered easily, and also that an innocent person might draw bad luck into his or her life by accidentally seeing a hostile witch or troubling an evil spirit.

Some apparently casual acts could also be dangerous, such as putting shoes on a table. In some places, it was said that putting shoes on the table would foretell a quarrel, or even the death of the owner. There are, of course, good reasons for the association of bad luck and shoes on a table. Shoes have been out of doors and have trodden on unclean things, and so placing them on a table could spread germs to food. It is no wonder that people believed that death would come to the house after such unhygienic practices.

Walking under ladders is another practice quite reasonably considered to be bad luck, because someone working above could drop something on you. Stepping on a crack is also considered bad luck for good reason, since anything cracked is likely also to be uneven and weak. Stepping on a crack could cause the ground to open or trip you and make you fall.

The number 13 was always considered the number of death. Even in Babylonian times, their leap year had a thirteenth month called the "month of the unlucky raven." The superstition about unlucky 13 also stems from the "Last Supper" when thirteen people sat at the table. To avoid bad luck at a dinner party, never seat thirteen people at a table. Ancient Romans also hated thirteen, seeing it as the number of death and destruction.

Friday the thirteenth is considered a very ill-favored day, with many considering it wise to avoid going out or traveling on that day. The thirteenth of the month is the worst day to start any new enterprise or to get married, so keep these plans for another day. To avoid bad luck, hotels rarely have a room thirteen or a thirteenth floor. If you have the misfortune to find yourself in such a room or floor, it may be wise to ask for alternative accommodation.

Breaking a mirror is also thought to bring seven years bad luck. Once, people believed that the soul was visible as a shadow or a reflection, and could be separated from the body without causing death. So long as the separated soul was unharmed or remained unbroken in a reflection, then it was safe. If the reflection was harmed in any way, then misfortune or death could follow. So, if you were using a mirror and dropped it, then your soul was thought to have suffered damage, and this was very unlucky.

"ONE LEAF FOR FAME
AND ONE LEAF FOR WEALTH
AND ONE FOR A FAITHFUL LOVER
AND ONE TO BRING YOU GLORIOUS HEALTH
ARE ALL IN A FOUR-LEAF CLOVER."

The four-leaf clover is one of the most powerful tools against bad luck. Finding a four-leaf clover is very lucky, and if the finder gives the four-leaf clover to someone else, their luck will increase. Here is a lovely old incantation that you should say for luck, if you find a four-leaf clover:

"One leaf for fame
And one leaf for wealth
And one for a faithful lover
And one to bring you glorious health
Are all in a four-leaf clover."

Spitting or spittle was a potent agent of magic and protection. If you wished to avert misfortune, then you spat in the direction from which evil came. If people wished to make a pact with someone, to show honesty and to avoid bad luck, they spat upon their hands before they shook hands. Children still sing this rhyme when they spit on one finger and make a deal with a friend:

"Wet finger wet
Dry finger dry
Cross my throat and hope to die
Should I ever tell a lie."

If you want to counteract the bad luck caused by walking under a ladder, you should cross your fingers and keep them crossed until you see a dog. Another method is to spit three times through the rungs of the ladder. Another charm expects you to spit on your shoe and then walk along and never look back till the spittle has dried.

If you believed that bad luck had entered your life, then you could always go to a mystic, a wise woman or a priest to get a talisman. Sometimes a talisman consisted of a piece of sacred material, such as a piece of wood, bone or material from a saint's body or coffin. Sometimes a piece of communion wafer spirited away from the church would also help. Ashes from sacred bonfires held at Beltane, Midsummer or Halloween also had protective powers. These ashes were scattered over fields to bring good crops, or placed in houses as protection. Ashes from these fires, put inside shoes, preserved the wearer from any great sorrow.

At home, there were some easily obtained good luck charms. A chicken's breastbone was considered very lucky and carried as a charm against misfortune. A well-known luck-charm is for two people to take the wishbone by the ends and pull it apart. The person who gets the bigger part of the bone can make a secret wish, as long as they never laugh or speak during the proceedings.

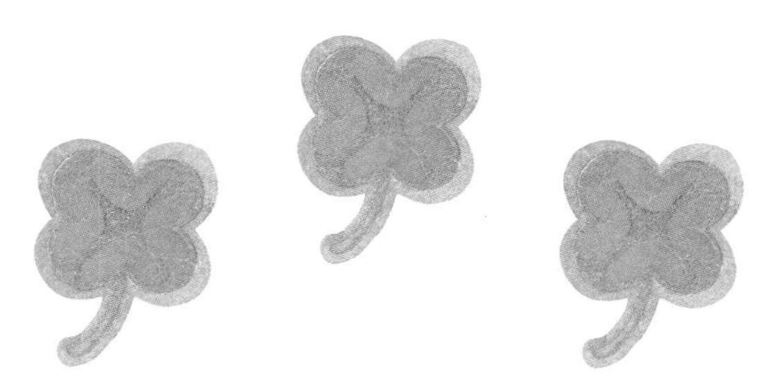

Ancient Beliefs: Modern Profits

Wealth and Superstitions

Wealth doesn't always take the form of money. Wealth can be a collection of great personal skills or talents, or having an abundance of happiness and health. Despite this, most people want to be successful with business ventures, improve their money situation, win a lottery, inherit money or find gold. Many charms or mascots have been created during history that are supposed to improve the chances of increasing your wealth. Most of the superstitions regarding these charms have come from the legends surrounding the ancient gods. Apollo the sun god and the goddess Fortuna, from whose name we take the word "fortune," were patrons of business and success. Ganesha, the Indian elephant god, has powers over wisdom, business and fortune, and people still pay homage to him before they enter into a business deal. The interesting thing about superstitions regarding wealth, money and profit, is that any charm or spell used to bring fortune will only work if the person using them is honest.

Disasters, or the gods, easily take material possessions away, and people have looked for protective charms to help them keep their worldly goods safe. The cornucopia is a charm that protects people in business. This charm, sometimes called the "Horn of Plenty," was sacred to various goddesses, such as Fortuna, Demeter, and Hathor, all of whom were responsible for the health and prosperity of the land. The cornucopia charm is usually made of silver or gold and worn on a bracelet or necklace. Sometimes it is painted over the door of a shop to ensure that plenty of success and fortune will shower upon the people the goddesses protect.

Abraxas stones were talismans in medieval Europe. They stood for saintly virtue and worldly success and were carried by businessmen. The abarax was a creature with the head of the cock, for watchfulness; the body of a man carrying a shield of wisdom and a whip of power, and snakes for legs, which stood for sense and understanding.

Various brooches and charms made of gold in the shape of honey bees have been worn since Grecian days as talismans for success in business and the increase of money. The Barberini Popes used the bees as their heraldic symbol. The honeybee was always known as a hard worker, and its golden treasure was symbolic of wealth and success. Therefore, it is considered very lucky if a honeybee hums near your head, as it is a foreteller of success. It is unlucky to hurt a bee or drive it away for this also drives away your fortune. If a swarm of bees comes to your house, and no one comes to claim them, then this is very unlucky, and misfortune will come to the house.

People in ancient Persia wore an agate as a charm to confer a fortune, especially through a legacy. They also believed that the stone would help to find buried treasure. In Europe, lucky florins and lucky sixpences, which had a cross on them, were kept in the belief that they would drive away the devil of poverty. Today, people can use silver or gold coins as talismans for financial gain, as long as they place a lucky mark upon them.

Grasshopper and cricket talismans are also lucky to wear for success in business and to bring good fortune. Hearing a cricket chirping is considered very good luck for any day's work. If one comes to the house, this is even luckier. Never kill a cricket or a grasshopper or this will kill your luck.

If you wish, you could try this old rhyme for gaining a lucky win or a gift. When the new moon is seen for the first time, greet it with three bows and say the following verse:

"New Moon, New Moon, first time I've seed 'ee,
Hope before the week's out, I'll have sommat gived to me."

"NEW MOON, NEW MOON, FIRST TIME I'VE SEED 'EE, HOPE BEFORE THE WEEK'S OUT, I'LL HAVE SOMMAT GIVED TO ME."

Many other superstitions were thought to help gain financial reward, and may still be lucky today. You may like to try them:
If you hear the first cuckoo of spring, you must make a wish and turn the money in your pocket, so it will grow.

Eating the first strawberries, or meeting a man with a straw hat, on the first day of summer is also very fortunate for gaining financial rewards, as long as you say the following rhyme immediately while touching both elbows and touching both hands:

"STRAWBERRY MAN,
STRAWBERRY MAN,
BRING ME GOOD LUCK
TODAY OR TOMORROW
TO PICK
SOMETHING UP."

"Strawberry man, strawberry man,
Bring me good luck
Today or tomorrow
To pick something up."

Then pick up a small stone or object and throw it over your left shoulder. Good fortune will come to you in the way of a lucky find or unexpected gift.
Never throw out your Christmas tree or take down your decorations before Twelfth Night. To throw your Christmas greenery out prematurely would be to throw away prosperity.

Springwort is a magical plant that was valued in ancient Greece and Rome, and in medieval times. If you pick some, it will give you the power to find hidden treasure and open locked doors.

If you wish to find lost gold, then take a sprig of yew and hold it out before you. The yew will lead you straight to where the lost treasure lies, and the branch will turn in your hand to direct you.

Should you ever find the end of a rainbow, you will also find a pot of gold.

Protecting your Investments

If you move to a new house or start a new business, you should be careful about which day is the best, for an old rhyme says:

"Monday for health
Tuesday for wealth
Wednesday's the best day of all
Thursday for crosses
Friday for losses
And Saturday's the worst day of all."

These superstitions may also help to start your new business off on a good foot:

- If you are stepping over the door of a new business premises, you must use your right foot first, as this will bring good luck to your business.
- If you are building new premises, place a gold coin in the foundations to bring prosperity and growth to your business.
- In China, a plant called the "jade tree," which is a small shrub with rounded, jade-colored leaves, is considered to be a very lucky plant to have growing outside your front door. There is a saying: "Jade by the door, poor no more."
- Never sweep dust out the door or you will sweep out your good fortune and your money.
- If the palm of your right hand itches, then money is coming. If it is the left hand that itches, you will lose money.
- The first red robin seen in winter will assure that a fortune is yours.
- A rabbit's foot is a well-known lucky charm, carried to bring success in every field.
- If you tread in manure, this is considered very lucky and predicts a growth in business.

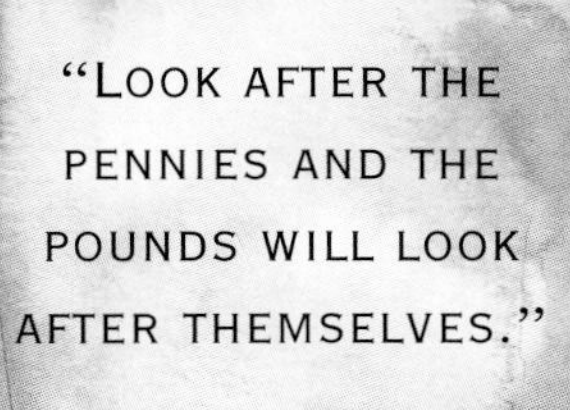

There is a lovely superstition regarding spiders. Romans often carried gold or silver talismans with spiders carved on them for success and fortune or to help with anything to do with trade.

The little spiders we see today, which we call money spiders, are the living representatives of this old custom. It is commonly believed that to kill a spider will cause misfortune and monetary loss. Seeing a spider in the house in the afternoon is lucky and is supposed to represent the sign of a gift arriving soon. If you dream of a spider, this is fortunate and means money and success are coming. If the spider bites you in the dream, it means you will lose money.

When it comes to money, there are a few contradictory old wives' tales. "A penny wise is a pound foolish," means that it doesn't pay to "penny pinch"as selfish people never prosper. Yet another saying counsels: "Look after the pennies and the pounds will look after themselves." This means that a prudent person can do well by saving sensibly.

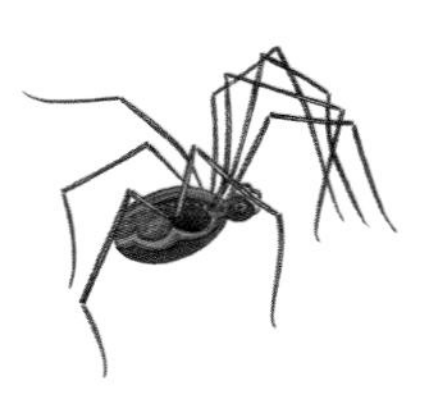

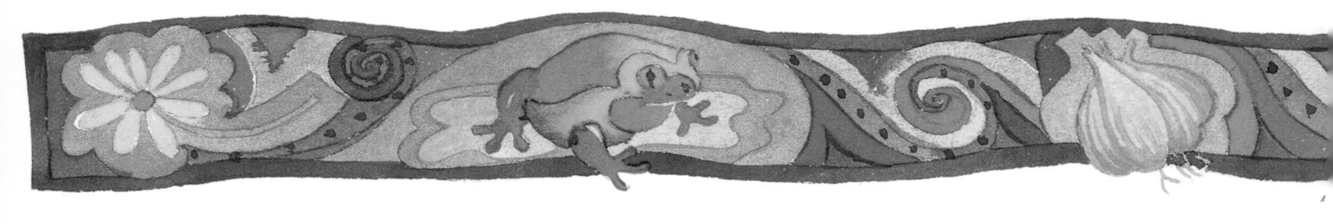

HEALTH AND WELL-BEING

INCANTATIONS FOR HEALTH

Health and well-being are our greatest gifts, we need these treasures to live a happy life. Unfortunately, plagues and diseases have always trouble mankind, and people have turned to magicians, doctors, shamans, faith healers, plants and animals and the gods for help in times of disease. In ancient Babylonian time, magicians or shamans delivered aid to the sick and prayed to Ea, the God of the Deep and the Lord of Light. Here is one spell used by a magician from 3,000 BC, which was said to help with curing the sick:

"I am the sorcerer priest of Ea
I come to revive the sick man
The great lord Ea has sent me;
He has added his pure spell to mine,
He has added his pure voice to mine,
He has added his pure spittle to mine."

It was believed in those times that the god's spittle was sacred and healing. It was also thought that the gods, both good and evil, wept creative tears. Those tears that fell from the eyes of evil gods created poisonous plants and animals, while the tears from the more benevolent deities created nourishing fruits and foods. Even in Christian mythology, it was believed that Satan created garlic and onions when he stepped out of the Garden of Eden after the fall of Adam and Eve. His left footprint caused garlic to spring up and his right, onions. Everything on earth belonged to the gods, and people dedicated the various

charms, incantations, plants and animals to the gods, and used them as "medicines."

An old country superstition to cure disease was to take a suffering patient outside when there was a new moon, blow on himor her nine times and say:

"What I see, may it increase,
What I feel, may it decrease
In the name of the Father, Son and Holy Ghost."

Another cure for disease was to catch the moon's rays in a dry silver dish and wash your hands in it, saying:

"I wash my hands in this thy dish,
O man in the moon, do grant my wish,
And come and take this away."

"I WASH MY HANDS
IN THIS THY DISH,
O MAN IN THE MOON,
DO GRANT MY WISH,
AND COME AND TAKE
THIS AWAY."

To help with poor vision, this poem by Longfellow may help:

"Above the lower plants it towers
The Fennel with its yellow flowers
And in an earlier age than ours
Was gifted with the wondrous powers
Lost vision to restore."

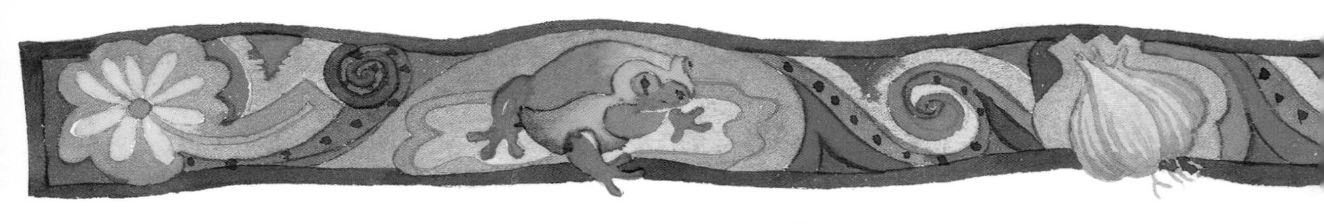

A medieval cure for a sty in the eye required a person to stroke the sty with a black cat's tail, drawing the tail downwards over the sty while saying the following incantation:

"I poke thee, I don't poke thee,
I poke the queff that's under the eye
O qualyway, O qualyway."

During the dark ages of Europe, charms were made from nearly anything. Any plant or animal that protected a person from malevolent witches meant it also protected against illness. Holding a cat's skin to the face was also supposed to be a remedy for toothache. Stroking a wart with a tortoiseshell cat's tail was supposed to cure warts.

Frogs in particular were singled out for some terrible spells. Rubbing a frog across the warts, and then impaling the frog on a thorn tree to die, was supposed to cure warts. A cure for thrush was to hold a frog in a patient's mouth. While it breathed, it breathed in the disease. Luckily, the frog was let go afterwards. It was also believed that a dried body of a frog worn in a silk bag around the neck averted epilepsy.

The ash tree was also considered a sacred tree that was supposed to protect people against evil spells, as well as helping to cure rickets and whooping cough. To cure whooping cough, a lock of hair was cut from the sufferer and attached to the tree. To cure warts, pins were stuck into the tree, then pulled out and stuck into the warts, using one pin for each wart. The pin was then returned to the tree. To cure rickets, an ash sapling was split in half and the affected child was passed nine times through the tree. The tree was then bound up, and if it healed, so would the child.

"RING A ROUND
THE ROSY,
A POCKET FULL
OF POSY.
ASHES, ASHES,
WE ALL FALL DOWN."

During the dark ages of Europe, the plant "rue" was thought to protect against all evil. It strengthened the sight, cured the bites of serpents and kept the plague away, so people wore posies of rue and fragrant plants around their necks. Unfortunately, it rarely worked as a ward against plague, and the red fevered cheeks and sneezes still appeared. This old superstition of keeping posies to ward off illness is kept alive today in the children's song:

"Ring around a rosy,
A pocket full of posy.
Ashes, ashes,
We all fall down."

Despite the fact that rue didn't help with the plague, it is still considered very useful as a liver and blood cleanser, and is used by contemporary herbalists today.

Even today we say, "an apple a day keeps the doctor away." This rhyme comes from the seventeenth century, when people also said: "To eat an apple before going to bed, will make a doctor beg his bread."

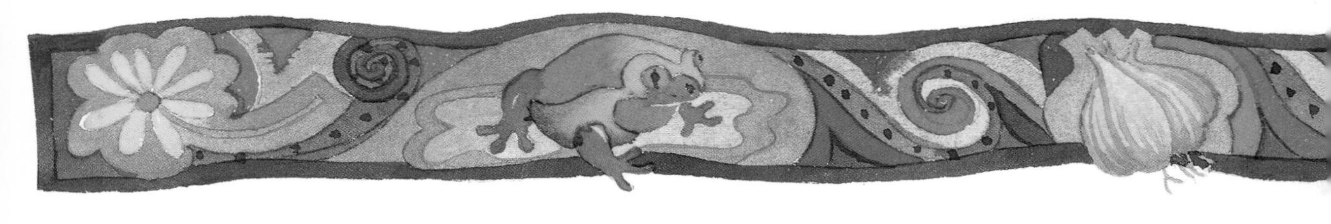

Warding off Illness

Nothing can ward off illness better than a healthy diet, plenty of exercise and good nights' sleep. Even in the old days, medicine men of all traditions recognized these important facts. Unfortunately, a range of diseases still manage to spoil our lives from time to time, so many methods have been devised to try to keep the pain and suffering of illness away. Good sleep is very important if you wish to remain healthy. This old rhyme was used for good sleep, along with an agrimony leaf put under the pillow:

"If it be ley'd under mann's head,
He shal' sleepyn as he were dead.
He shal never drede ne wakyn,
Till fro under his head it be taken."

Keys were very old amulets symbolizing the key to wisdom, to the heart and to life. Three keys were used as a charm by the Japanese to unlock the doors leading to love, health and wealth, and were kept for general fortune and well-being.

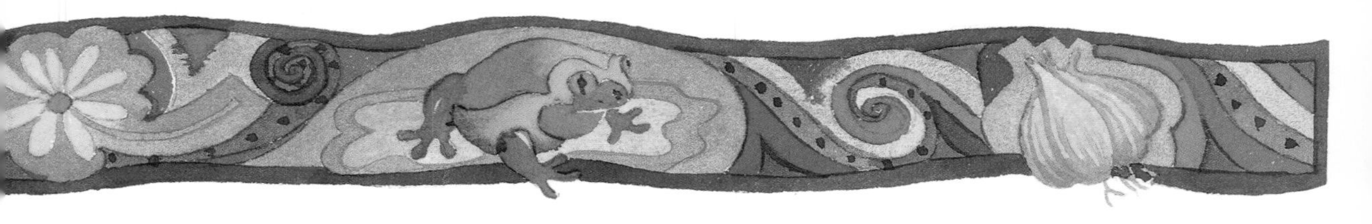

If you wish to ward off ill health, never cut your nails on a Sunday, for if you do, you will have the Devil with you all week.

Cobwebs were once used to stop the bleeding in minor cuts. Rolled into pills, it was believed they relieved the ague and asthma, and helped restless people sleep.

A potato was used to help ward off the pain from arthritis. To do this, a potato was cut in half and kept in the pocket until it shriveled away, the idea being that the pain would similarly wither. This old cure is still used by a number of people, as is the use of a copper bangle worn on the affected limb to keep the pain away.

This 4,000-year-old prayer to Asclepius, a mortal Greek physician who became the god of healing, may also be of help to those who are feeling depressed:

"Physician of Illness!
Asclepius, son of Apollo!
In the beginning I sing.
I [insert your name] who was born on the Dotian Plain [insert place of birth].
You give to mankind a great joy.
You charm away painful afflictions.
Thus Lord I hail you,
And with my singing entreat you to bring me happiness."

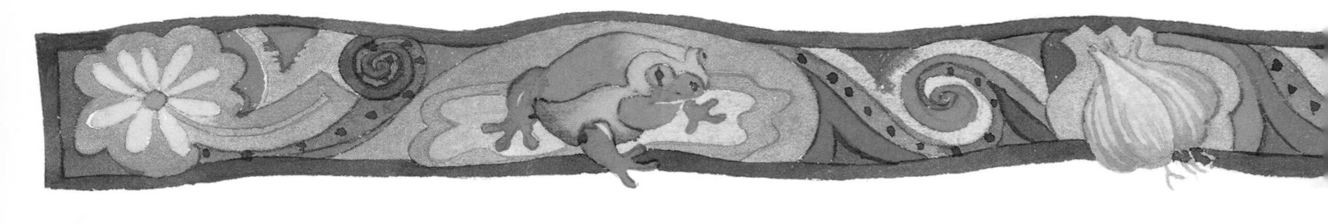

Burning sacred oils and incense helped take prayers to the gods, and created a general sense of well-being. Frankincense and myrrh were also some of the oldest herbs used to create good health and happiness. Burning incense or plant oils is still an excellent way of relaxing and focusing on good thoughts and happiness.

Herbs, such as sandalwood, jasmine and lavender, are fragrant herbs for inducing a sense of serenity. The scent of sandalwood is relaxing, and it has traditionally been used as a sedative and an aphrodisiac. Jasmine and lavender both have the ability to relax and work as anti-depressants to invigorate the spirits. Jasmine works particularly well for alleviating stress, fatigue, irritability and apathy.

The flame of a candle has also inspired long-held superstitions regarding health and well-being. The candle was used in sacred lore and burned in temples and churches, symbolizing change, purification and sacrifice. The colors of the candles were also considered to be magically significant. Try burning an orange candle for a sense of assertiveness and endurance; a gold

candle for success in business; a blue candle for inner peace and tranquility; and a lilac candle for relaxation and restful sleep.

Happiness is a very difficult emotion to capture in our days of stress and hard work. Many people suffering from depression and looking for ways to improve their lifestyles turn to traditional charms and superstitions, which were supposed to help with finding happiness.

Wearing a wild pansy was an old charm for "gladdening the heart," because the wild pansy, or heart's ease, was a plant dedicated to the "Trinity," because it had three colors.

St John's Wort, hypericum was believed in medieval times to ward off fairies. A superstition also said it was sacred to the female spirits: mares or maers. The maers lived in the wild woodlands and settled on sleepers, choking off their breath. This is the derivation of the word "nightmare." Wise women have long used the plant to treat insomnia caused by depression and anxiety attacks. Even today, it is particularly useful in restoring a zest for life in older people who may feel lonely or cast aside.

It was also said that St John would appear in a dream if you placed hypericum in a pillow and slept on it overnight. It was believed the plant would give you his blessing and protection for the coming year.

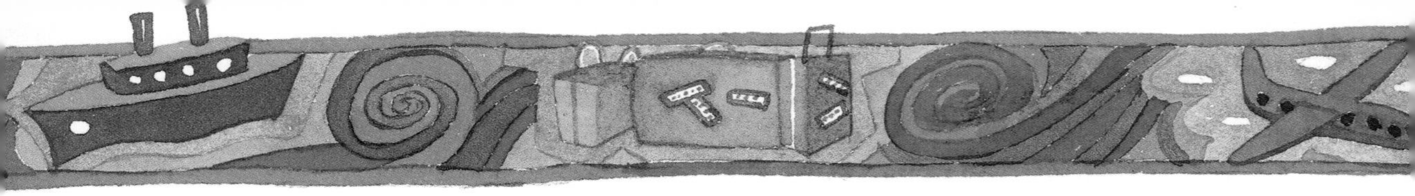

TRAVEL

TRAVEL SUPERSTITIONS

In days of old, few maps existed, roads were poor, wild animals and robbers waited to attack travelers and few safe places to rest could be found along the way. Traveling was not taken lightly; most people who set out on a journey did so with great trepidation. For those who traveled by land, dangerous animals and malevolent witches caused problems. People thought that if a hare, black cat, flat-footed person or shrew crossed their path during a journey, then the journey was doomed. The traveler could cancel this bad luck by returning home, sitting down and counting to nine, ten or twenty. The traveler was also supposed to eat and drink something while at home. Afterwards, he or she could start a new journey, hopefully one with better omens.

Sea voyages were equally dangerous, and many a sailor and ship were lost. Sailors were particularly superstitious and considered many omens as ominous. If a sailor lost a mop or bucket over the side during a sea-journey, he believed his luck went with it. Sharks following a ship were also considered very bad luck, as people believed sharks could smell death, so a death would shortly occur. Sailors were careful never to hurt an albatross during a sailing trip. If a sailor killed an albatross, the bird was hung around his neck until it rotted off. The saying "He's got an albatross around his neck" is used when a person has a run of terrible luck.

Sailors also think it is very unlucky to change the name of a ship. In the old days, if a vessel had to be renamed, it had to be refitted. This meant the old mast had to be burned. Later, it was considered safe merely to stick a nail

or a knife into the existing mast. Later again, a lucky coin was placed under the mast for good luck. During the refit, all references to the ship's old name had to be removed from documents, life-vests and lifeboats. When the newly named craft was relaunched, the sailors asked Neptune (god of the sea) and Aeolus (god of the winds) to forget the previous name of the craft, and accept the name of the new ship.

It was considered very unlucky to call a boat anything like "Wave Master" or "Storm Rider" because this was thought to be boasting, which would tempt the gods to destroy the craft. Once the ship was named successfully and the gods carefully and respectfully asked to bless the craft, expensive wine was poured over the port and starboard bows and people drank the health of the ship. Later, champagne was used to launch vessels.

HOLIDAY CHARMS AND SAFE-DRIVING AMULETS

Starting out on a journey or a holiday away from home should be the beginning of a happy time. However, any journey takes you away from all that is safe and comfortable. If you are worried about your journey, a few old superstitions may help you on your way. For instance, it was once believed that spitting on a person when they set out on a journey would bring them good luck.

Friday is a bad day to start any journey, especially Friday the thirteenth, but if you sneeze and turn your head to the right, this is a lucky start to any journey.

Also, if you see a black snail when leaving the house, grab it quickly by the horns, and throw it over your left shoulder for a lucky journey.

It was also believed that a lucky journey began with the right foot. Any journey started with the left foot was unlucky. It was also considered bad luck for any member of the family to watch after a traveler until they disappeared from sight. To look back when you started a journey, especially for fishermen who were setting out to sea, was thought to be umlucky. If a fisherman forgot something, he had to leave it behind unless one of his family ran after him and gave it to him from the front. Likewise, children of seamen made sure to crush their eggshells after eating a boiled egg, for there was a rhyme that said:

"Oh never leave your eggshells unbroken in a cup;
Think of the poor sailor men and always smash them up,
For witches come and find them and sail away to sea
And make a lot of misery for sailormen like me."

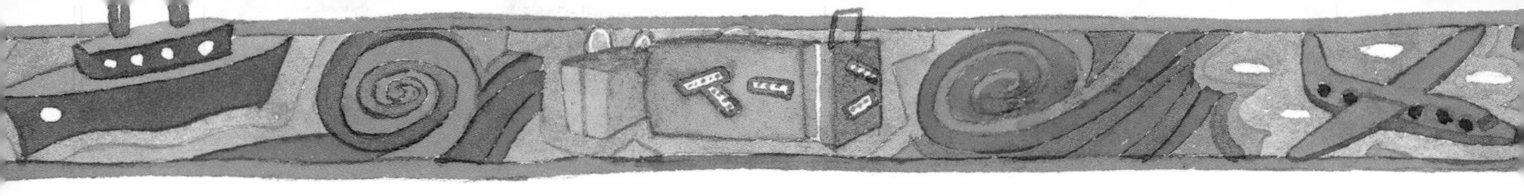

Cauls, or the birth membrane covering a child's head, are considered very lucky as mascots for travelers and protection for sailors against drowning. In the seventeenth century, midwives did a brisk trade in the sale of cauls, selling them to sailors and travelers as protective amulets.

Saint Christopher was the patron saint of travelers. He also was in charge of making sure that the souls of the dead traveled safely to the afterlife. Medals depicting St Christopher have been carried for centuries as talismans for safe travel, and they are often seen hanging from the rear vision mirrors of cars.

Taxicab numbers also carry luck. Special lucky numbers should contain a seven, or a letter U because U resembles a horseshoe. This is also the case for car number plates.

ANIMALS

ANIMALS AND SUPERSTITIONS

Abundant evidence throughout the world shows that people have always considered animals to be highly spiritual. Many gods, goddesses and totemic deities had animal heads and body parts, such as the Hindu elephant god, Ganesha, the Egyptian jackal-headed god, Anubus, and the falcon-headed god, Horus.

Shamans, priests and other devotees of various faiths wore animal costumes and masks; they mimicked animals' actions in sacred dances, perhaps to ask for help with hunting, or so the shaman could emulate the animals' power and special abilities.

Demons and evil monsters also existed, which were created with animal horns, and tails. Evil spirits, fairies and shape changers all had the ability to change themselves into animals. Bats, toads, hares, shrews and black cats all had a sinister reputation. Witches were believed to be able to turn themselves into these creatures, and through the bewitched animal, they could cast evil spells and black magic, causing innocent people to suffer illness and misfortune.

Good nymphs and fairies also changed themselves into animals. The hare was once sacred to the moon goddess and to the goddess Eostre, from whom the name Easter was derived. This is why the amulet of the rabbit's foot is considered good luck.

In Cornwall, England, ants were supposedly very, very old fairies who had shriveled up, and were in the last stages of their earthly existence. It was considered very unlucky to kill ants.

The cicada, too, was once a handsome young man. The dawn goddess fell in love with him and bestowed immortality upon him. Unfortunately, she didn't bestow youth, and he shriveled up. He became ugly and she abandoned him. Now, only his voice can be heard as he greets his ex-lover, despairingly, in the morning. The sign or amulet of the cicada is the sign of a discarded lover.

Goats have been domesticated for centuries. The goat was sacred to Saturn (father of time). "Old Father Time" was often depicted wearing a goat's beard. The goat symbolized riches and wealth, along with the time and perseverance to create such things. The goat's horn is the horn of the cornucopia and symbolizes riches.

Scandinavian people played goat games, and made a Yule goat out of straw, which they burned. They also had a goat dance, which twirled around the straw goat. This is where we get the saying "acting the giddy-goat."

Lucky Animals

In many early religions, tribes or people identified themselves with a particular animal. Often, people belonged to animal totems, and avoided certain foods because of their belief in the sacredness of that animal. Other animals had special attributes, which people saw as unique, or lucky and these beliefs still exist today in the forms of various "lucky" animals.

Frogs were sacred to Egyptian midwives and the crone 'Hecate' wore a frog amulet with the words "I am the resurrection" inscribed upon it. The lion was sacred to the sun, as were the eagle and the rooster. The dove was sacred to Aphrodite. Ravens, vultures, jackals and dogs were associated with the underworld.

The scarab beetle was one of the oldest good luck charms as it was associated with regeneration and the sun. The beetle was carved on mummies, and appeared in most Egyptian iconography as a symbol of rebirth and joy.

Tortoises are also lucky. There was an oriental belief that the world was supported on the back of a tortoise. Tortoise amulets are supposed to confer long life and protection from the evil eye. The tortoise is also sacred to Mercury (Hermes) and is a symbol of a "peace maker." The charm is supposed to help make peace between enemies.

Robins are lucky birds to see. However, it is very unlucky to kill a robin, to steal or break its eggs or to disrupt its nest. Whoever does such a wicked thing will fall under the power of the worst variety of witches. If anyone breaks a robin's egg, then something he or she values will be broken in return.

The humble ladybird is thought to be a lucky insect. It is a sign of good fortune if it lands on you. Ladybirds must be allowed to fly away and not be brushed off. The deeper the red on the ladybird's back, the luckier it is. The number of spots on its back should also be counted because you will be lucky for as many months as there are spots. It is very unlucky to kill a ladybird.

Other superstitions surround many animals, meeting or seeing the following animals is supposed to bring luck:

- ★ The first white butterfly seen in spring is considered lucky.
- ★ The first lamb seen in spring is also lucky. If it is black, make a wish, knowing that any wish you make will be fulfilled.
- ★ It is lucky to meet a toad. To kill one brings down the rain or could cause a storm. Some terrible charms were made using toads, but all such dangerous spells had a habit of coming back to those who made them, thrice.

Many animals are cherished because of their beauty, their closeness to mankind or their wonderful history and symbolism. Birds were often seen as messengers from the gods bringing omens and enlightenment. Crows, vultures and ravens took the souls of the dead to the afterlife in the sky. Later, birds wings were attached to angels and fairies and other godly messengers.

The swan was very significant as a symbol of noble purity in the ancient world. Both male and female swan spirits appeared in pagan mythology. Zeus turned into a swan to seduce Leda, who mothered the heavenly twins, Castor and Pollux. Swan maidens were fairies who took off their feathers at night and bathed in lakes. It is still considered very unlucky to kill a swan. Tradition tells that swan eggs will only hatch during thunder and lightning, and that swans sing the most beautiful songs before they die, called "swan songs."

Before Noah's great flood, the kingfisher was a gray bird, but when it was released from the ark, it flew so high that its feathers turned blue, while its tail feathers were burned by the sun as it turned back to earth, which is why they are red.

It was believed that when kingfishers breed, there are no storms at sea and the weather is fine. Kingfishers' feathers and skin are never supposed to rot

and, therefore, are used to preserve any material they touch. For this reason housewives kept kingfishers' feathers in their linen. The peacock also had similar legends about its flesh, but it is very unlucky to bring the peacock's tail feathers indoors.

The magpie is a talkative bird credited with bringing good news or the news of visitors. If you see magpies or jackdaws, there is lovely rhyme you can say:

"One for sorrow, two for mirth.
Three for a letter, and four for a birth.
Five for silver, and six for gold.
Seven for a story that will never be told."

Strangely, snakes should not be feared or considered unlucky. From the earliest times, they have been thought of as the embodiment of enlightenment. The Kundalini spirit is depicted, in Indian tradition, as two snakes entwined along the spine. The snake was sacred at one time to Gaea (Mother Earth). Snakes' skins and snake-heads worn as amulets have always been associated with healing and good fortune. Snakes became evil after the stories of the serpent's role in the "Fall of Eden," but it should be remembered that the doctor's symbol of healing is still the "caduceus wand" which has two snakes entwined around a wand.

Animals to Avoid

Not all animals were considered lucky; some had a darker side. Devils, imps and evil spirits wore various animal horns and tails. Various monstrosities lived in hell with donkey's ears and goat legs, half human and half spirit. Werewolves and vampires haunted the darkness of the night, filling people's imagination with terror. Many animals such as owls, cats, bats, spiders and dogs had unearthly superstitions surrounding them.

Cerebus was a three-headed dog, which guarded the underworld Hades. Anubis, the jackal-headed Egyptian deity, made sure the souls of the dead arrived safely in the underworld. Bats were believed to be malevolent witches or vampires and were greatly and unjustly feared. Black beetles are still considered unlucky, and if they crawl over a person's shoe, this is a death omen. Hares should be avoided: there is a rhyme, which tells how a witch turns herself into a hare by saying:

"I shall go into a hare
With sorrow and sych meikle care:
And I shall go in the devil's name
Ay while I come home again."

Almost all night-animals, including owls, are considered unlucky. Owls were feared in Roman times and were associated with death and disaster. It is also common for people to hear "the owl call their name" which means they will die.

The house sparrow is not lucky. "The spink and the sparrow, are the Devil's bow and arrow," says an old rhyme. It was believed the sparrow betrayed

Christ in the garden of Gethsemane. It is a bad omen if a sparrow flies into a house, but it is also unlucky to kill one.

The crow and the raven are seen as birds of ill omen. To meet a single crow is considered very unlucky, and to hear one croaking on the left side, in the morning, is very unlucky. If a single crow flutters over you, or flutters outside the window of a house, then this is a death omen.

Foxes have always been associated with cunning and trickery. In Norse myth, the fox was associated with Loki, the god of trickery. Its reddish coat was associated with fire, and later with hell, which doomed the creature as one of the devil's followers. In ancient Rome, the fox was also considered a fire demon.

In Asian legends, the fox is endowed with a special talent for seduction and is especially lecherous. Magical fox women were supposed to seduce and steal the life force of men, thereby destroying them. In general, foxes are crafty deceivers, and foxes seen anywhere around a house warn of a coming death and disaster. Meeting several foxes at any time is very unlucky.

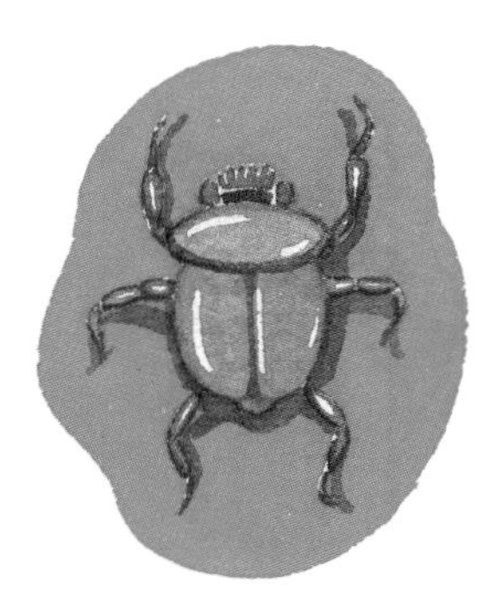

This edition published by Barnes & Noble, Inc.,
by arrangement with Lansdowne Publishing

2002 Barnes & Noble Books

ISBN 0-7607-3173-X

M 10 9 8 7 6 5 4 3 2 1

Commissioned by Deborah Nixon
Text: Eleanor Coombe
Illustrator: Sue Ninham
with additional illustrations by Penny Lovelock
Designer: Sue Rawkins
Editor: Antonia Beattie
Production Manager: Jane Kirby
Project Coordinator: Rea Hatzi-Fatouros

This book is intended to give general information only. The publishers expressly disclaim all liability to any person arising directly or indirectly from the use of, or for any errors or omissions in, the information in this book. The adoption and application of the information in this book is at the reader's discretion and is his or her sole responsibility.

Set in Stone Serif and Copperplate on QuarkXpress
Printed in Singapore by Tien Wah Press (Pte) Ltd